P IS FOR
President

by Wendy Cheyette Lewison
illustrated by Valerio Fabbretti

Grosset & Dunlap
An Imprint of Penguin Random House

For my amazing grandchildren, Josh and Leah—May you be
what you want to be. Even president—WCL

To my grandparents—VF

GROSSET & DUNLAP
Penguin Young Readers Group
An Imprint of Penguin Random House LLC

Text copyright © 2016 by Wendy Cheyette Lewison. Illustrations copyright © 2016 by Valerio Fabbretti.
All rights reserved. Published by Grosset & Dunlap, an imprint of Penguin Random House LLC,
345 Hudson Street, New York, New York 10014. GROSSET & DUNLAP is a trademark of
Penguin Random House LLC. Manufactured in China.

Library of Congress Cataloging-in-Publication Data is available.

ISBN 978-1-101-99611-9   10 9 8 7 6 5 4 3 2 1

P is for president—the president of
the United States of America.

Who is the president? The president is the leader of our country. He can come from any kind of family. He can be any color and any religion. He can be a she! But there are some rules. He must be at least thirty-five years old.

And he or she must be born an American citizen.

The president can also do any kind of work. Many of our presidents have been lawyers or teachers. Many have served in the military as soldiers. Some were farmers. One was an engineer. One was an inventor. One was even an actor!

What does the president do? The president has a hard job! He works to fix problems in America. He works to make sure you stay healthy and get a good education. He works to make peace in the world. He does a lot of listening. He shakes a lot of hands.

He has so much to do that he works day and night. A person must have a lot of energy to be president of the United States of America!

But the president doesn't work alone. He works with other people. The president tells them his ideas and listens to theirs. Then he tries to work things out with them. He is our leader, but he is not the boss of everyone!

How does someone get to be president? He works hard to learn about our country. He studies American history and what is happening in America today. When he decides to run for president, we call him a candidate.

The candidate goes all around the country and talks to people. We call this a campaign. During the campaign, he tries to show people that he is the right candidate for the job—the most important job in America!

When the campaign is over, people must decide who they think will do the best job—this candidate or that one? All across America, over a hundred million people go to the polls to vote, so they can help choose. When you are eighteen years old, you will be able to help pick the next president, too!

The winner of the election becomes our president for the next four years. He moves into the White House in Washington, DC, and the old president moves out. The White House is a big white house where all of our presidents—except the first, George Washington—have lived.

The new president's whole family lives in the White House with him. We call the president's family the First Family.

Many presidential pets have lived in the White House, too—dogs, cats, snakes, turkeys, goats, bears, and lizards. One president even had a pet alligator!

The White House is a big and busy place. There are 132 rooms and 32 bathrooms. Many people work there. Chefs cook meals. Housekeepers clean. There are personal assistants and government officials, too. The president doesn't get much privacy!

The president doesn't stay in the White House all the time. He travels a lot. He meets with people all over America and all around the world. He even has his own limousine, helicopter, and airplane.

But everywhere he goes, Secret Service agents are with him. They are there to protect him and keep him safe, so he can do the job given to him by the American people.

We have had many presidents since America became a nation hundreds of years ago. Some presidents have done such a good job for America that we want to remember them all the time. So we have named cities and streets after them. We have put their faces on our money.

We have built beautiful monuments.
Maybe someday you will visit them.
And maybe someday . . .

...the president will be YOU!